# THE LITTLE RED

# SHIRT

# COLORING BOOK

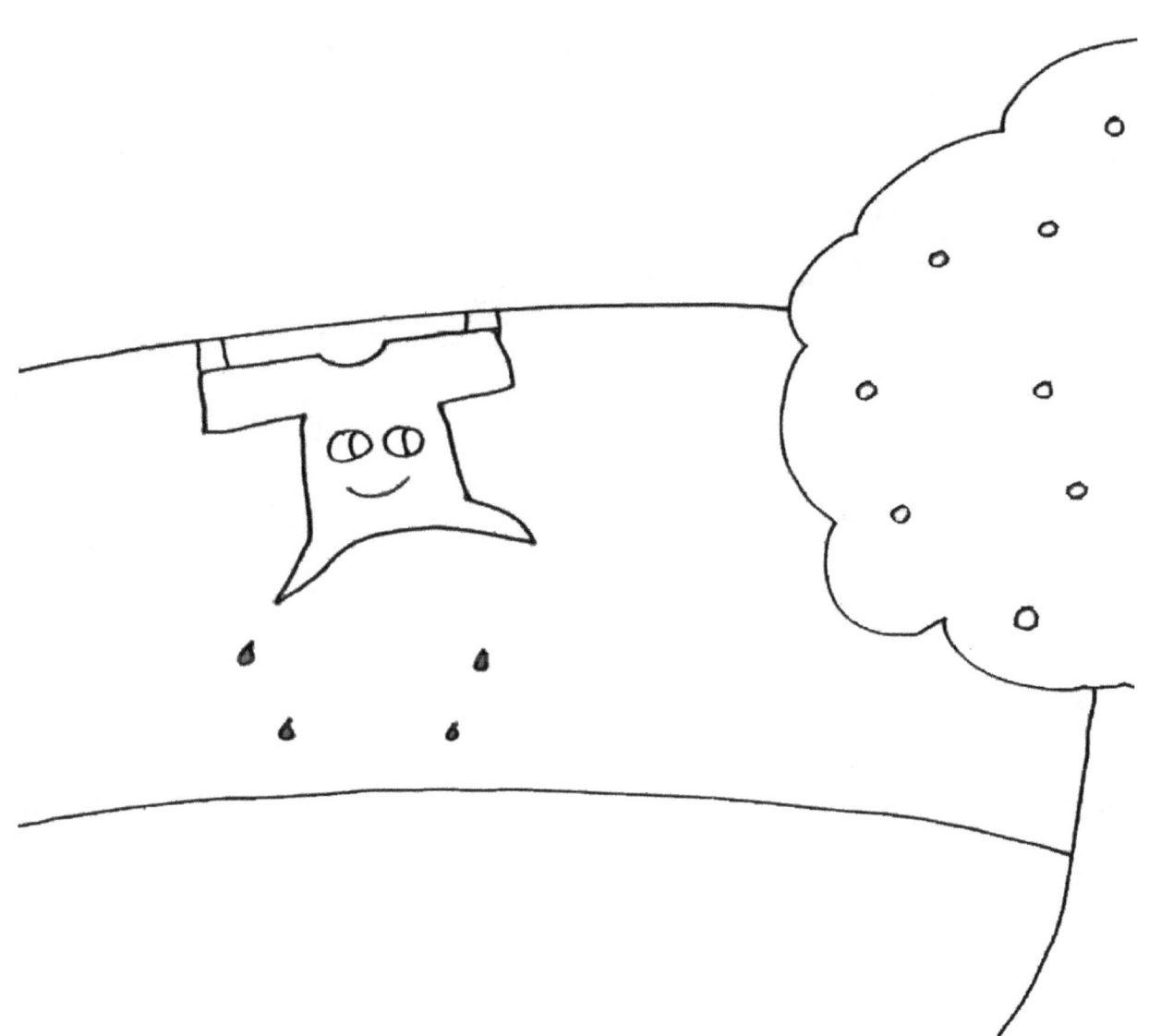

This book was created as a companion to the

## The Little Red Shirt

The pictures purposely do not have finite lines which will enable the colorist to extend the lines if desired.

Add your own pictures if you like and change the story!

Email:  favoritesofruthies@gmail.com

Join me on my Facebook Group:

Coloring Designs

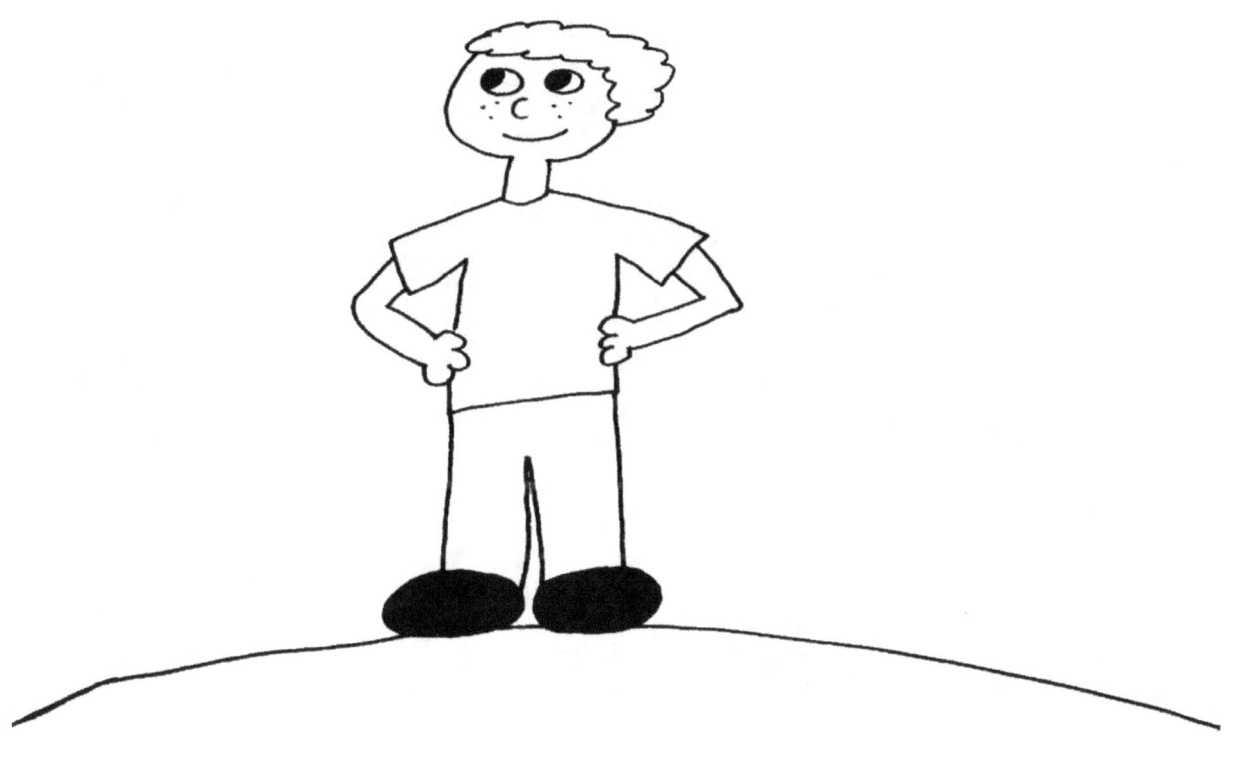

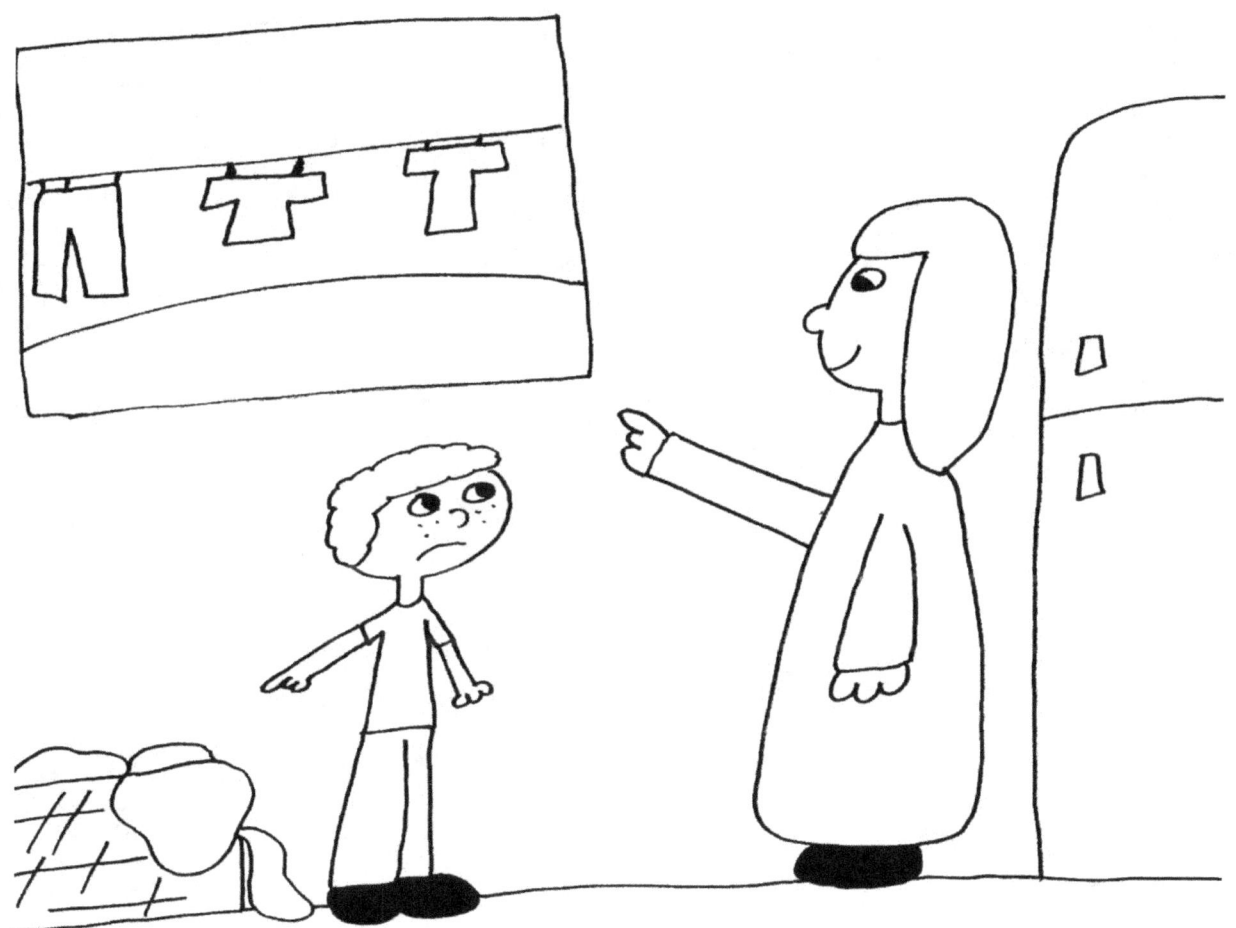

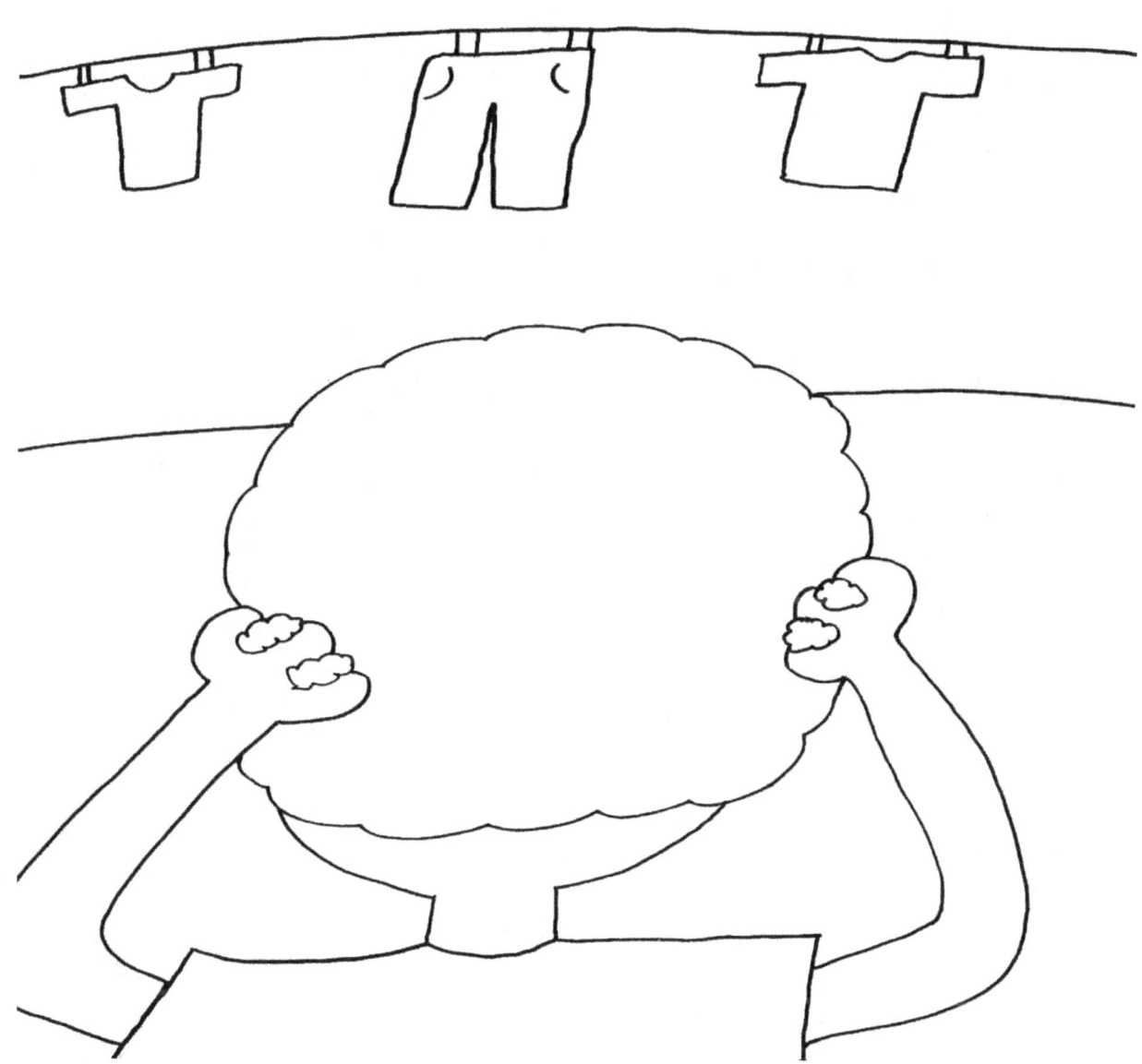

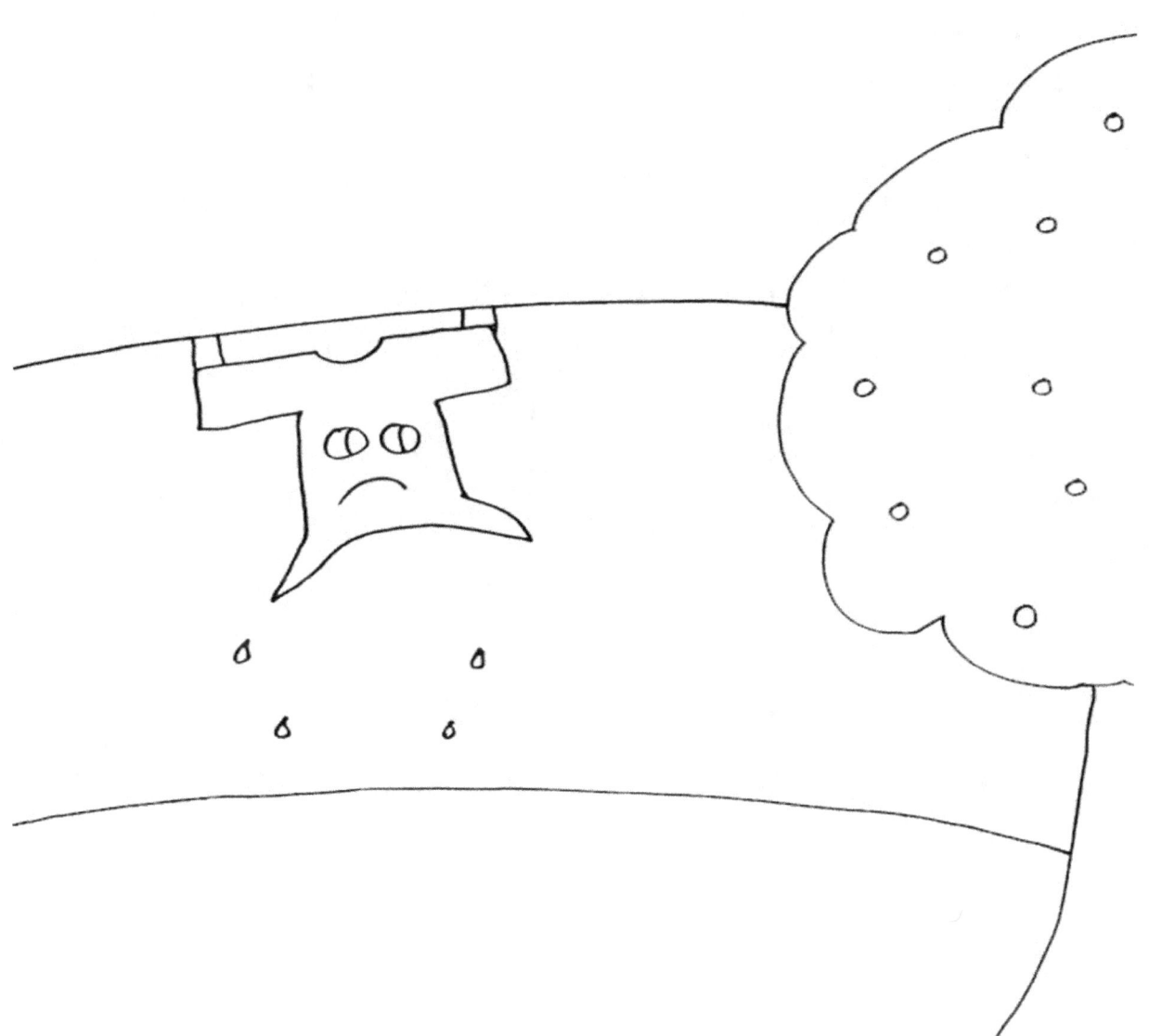

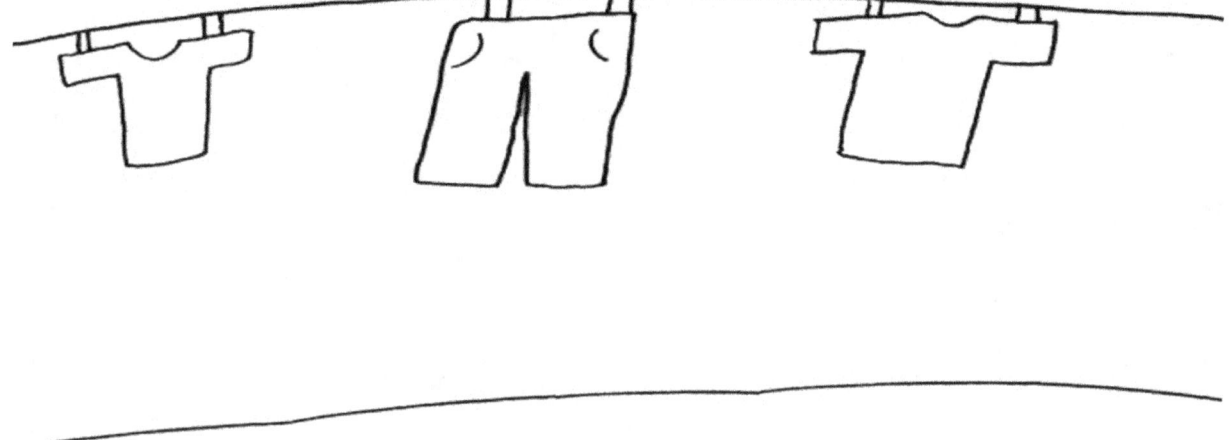

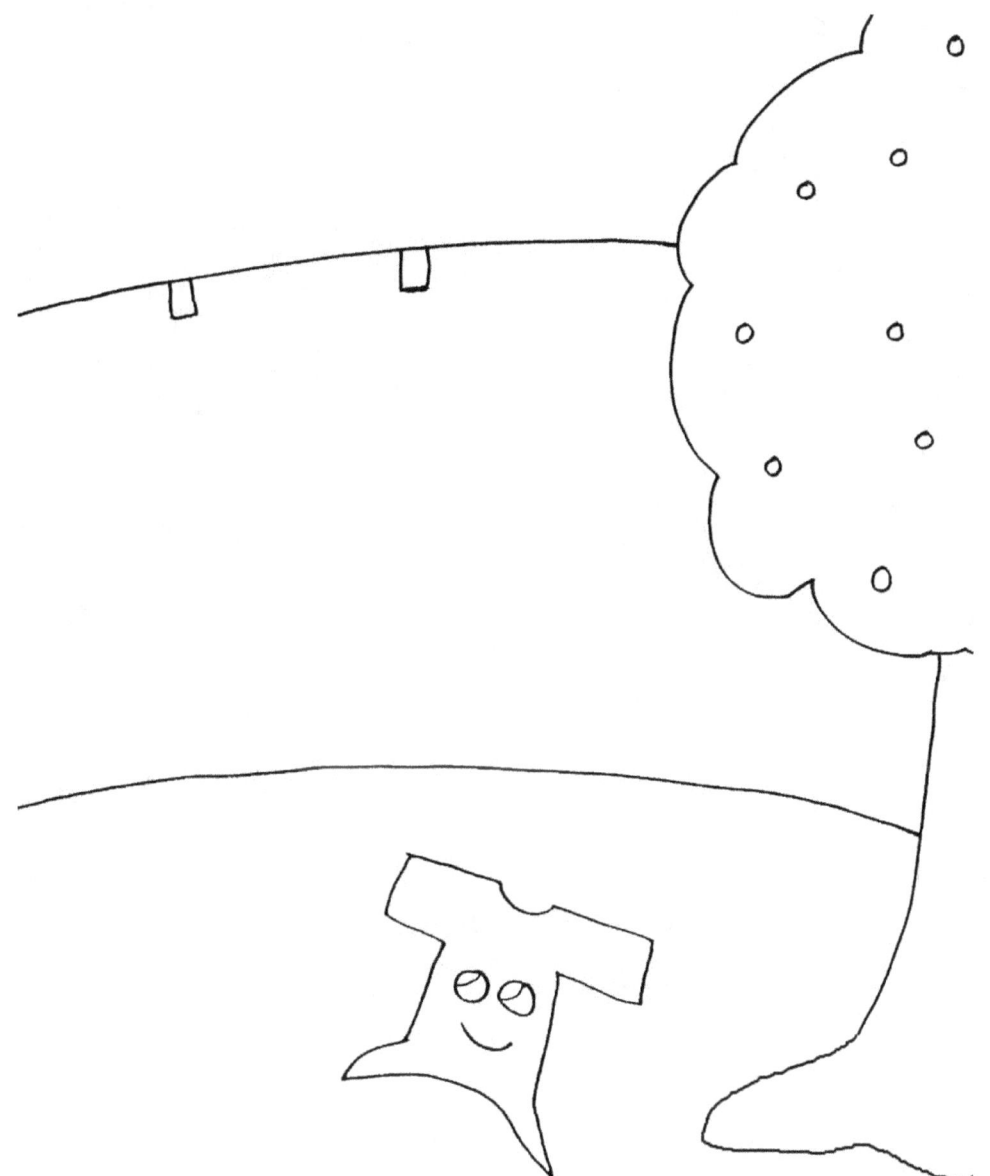

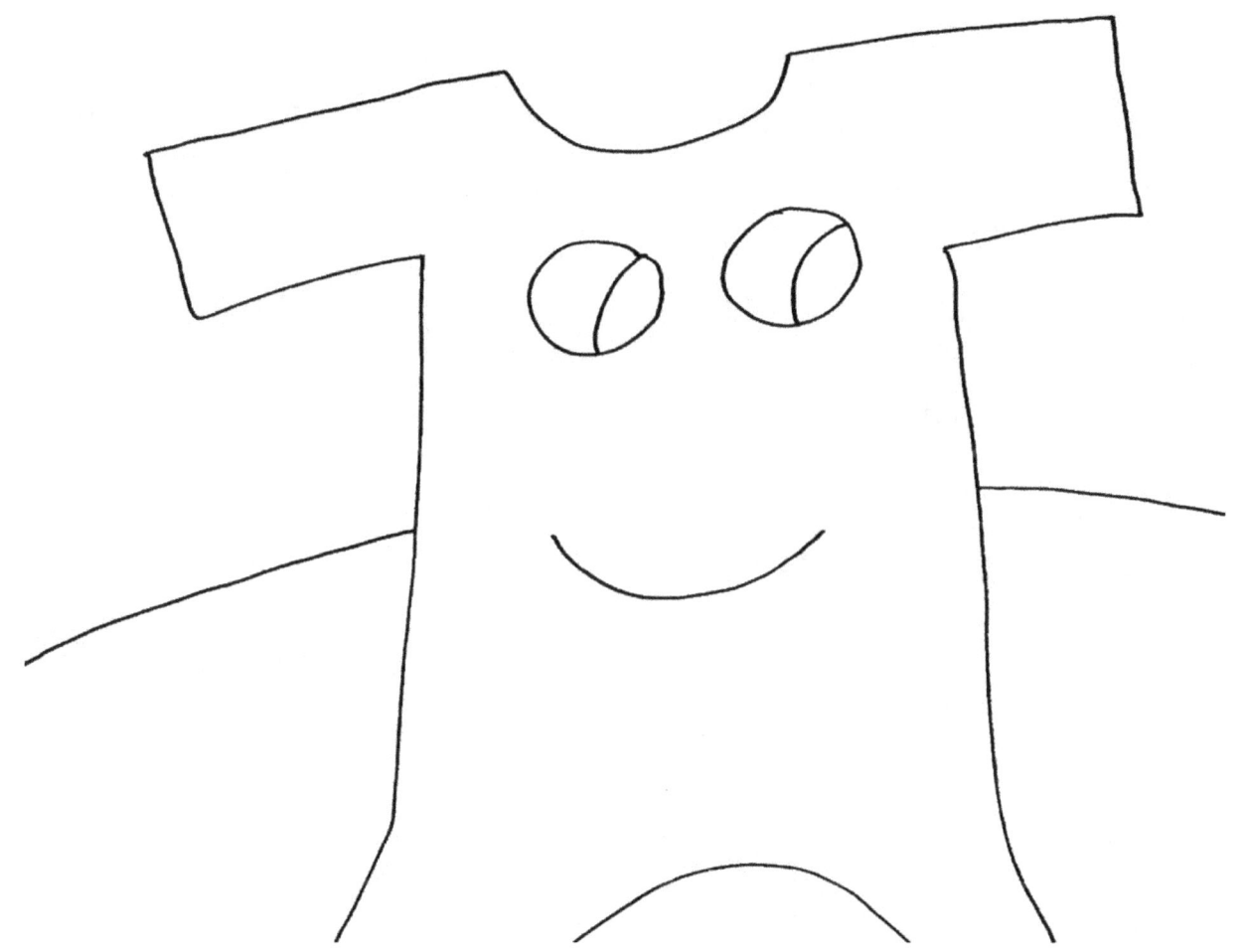

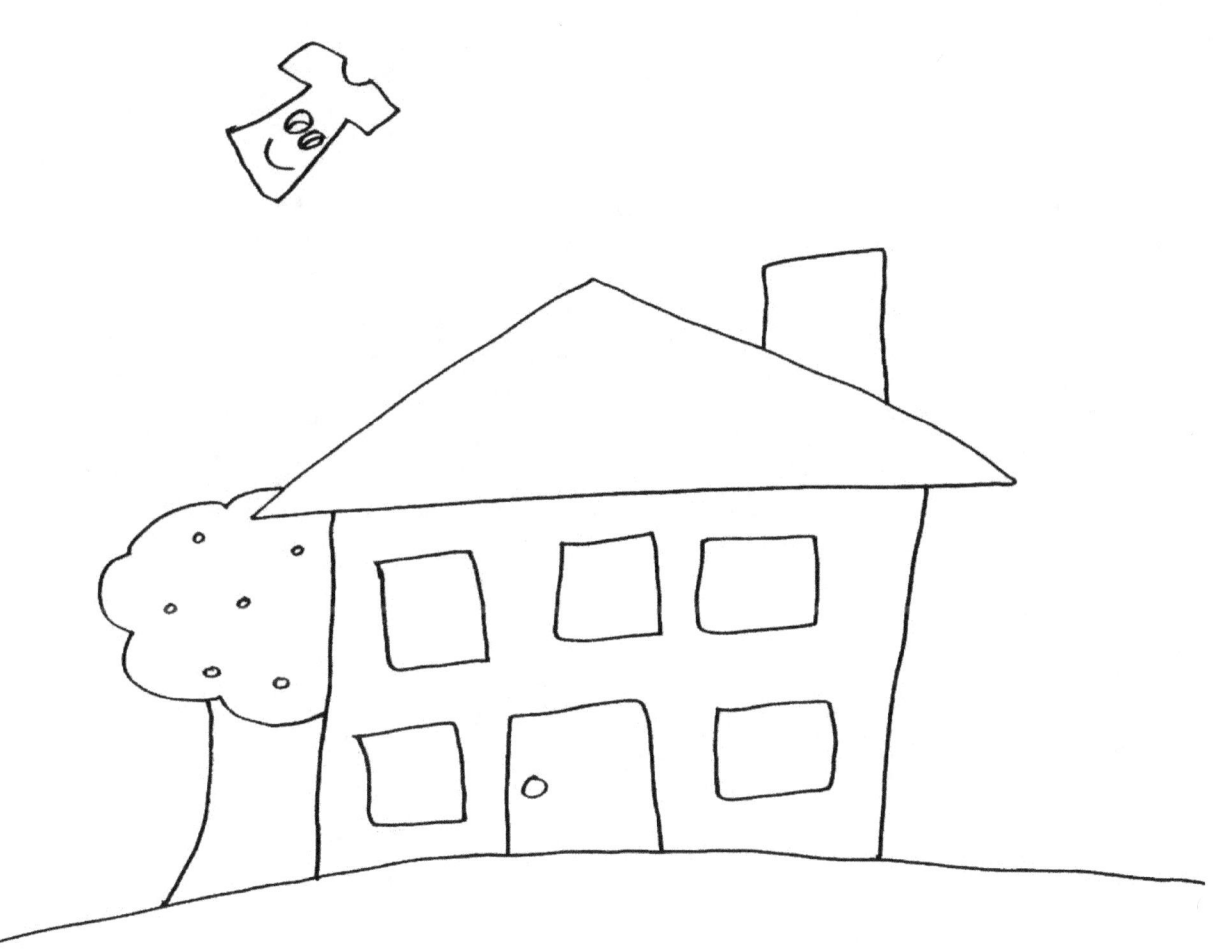

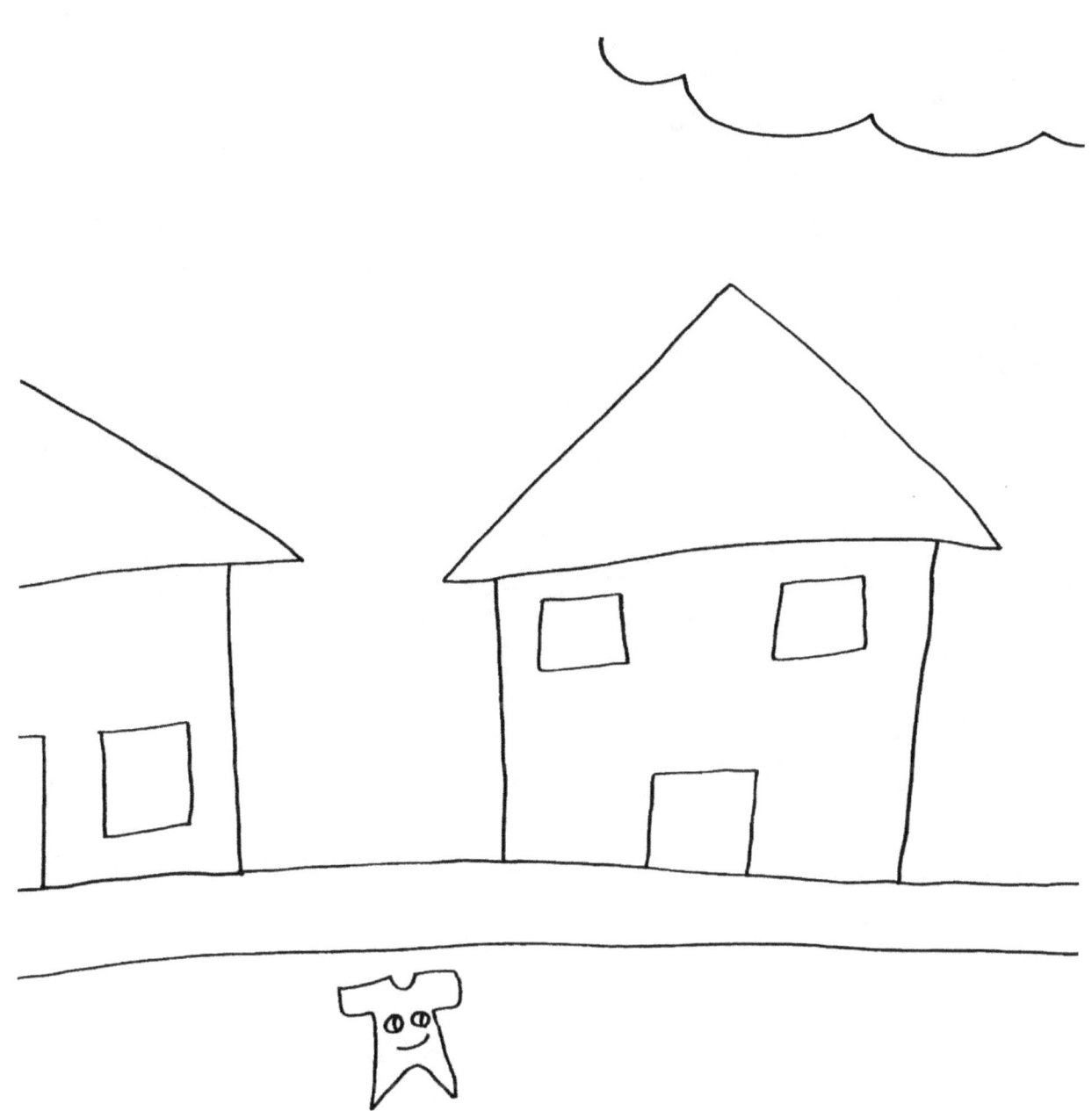

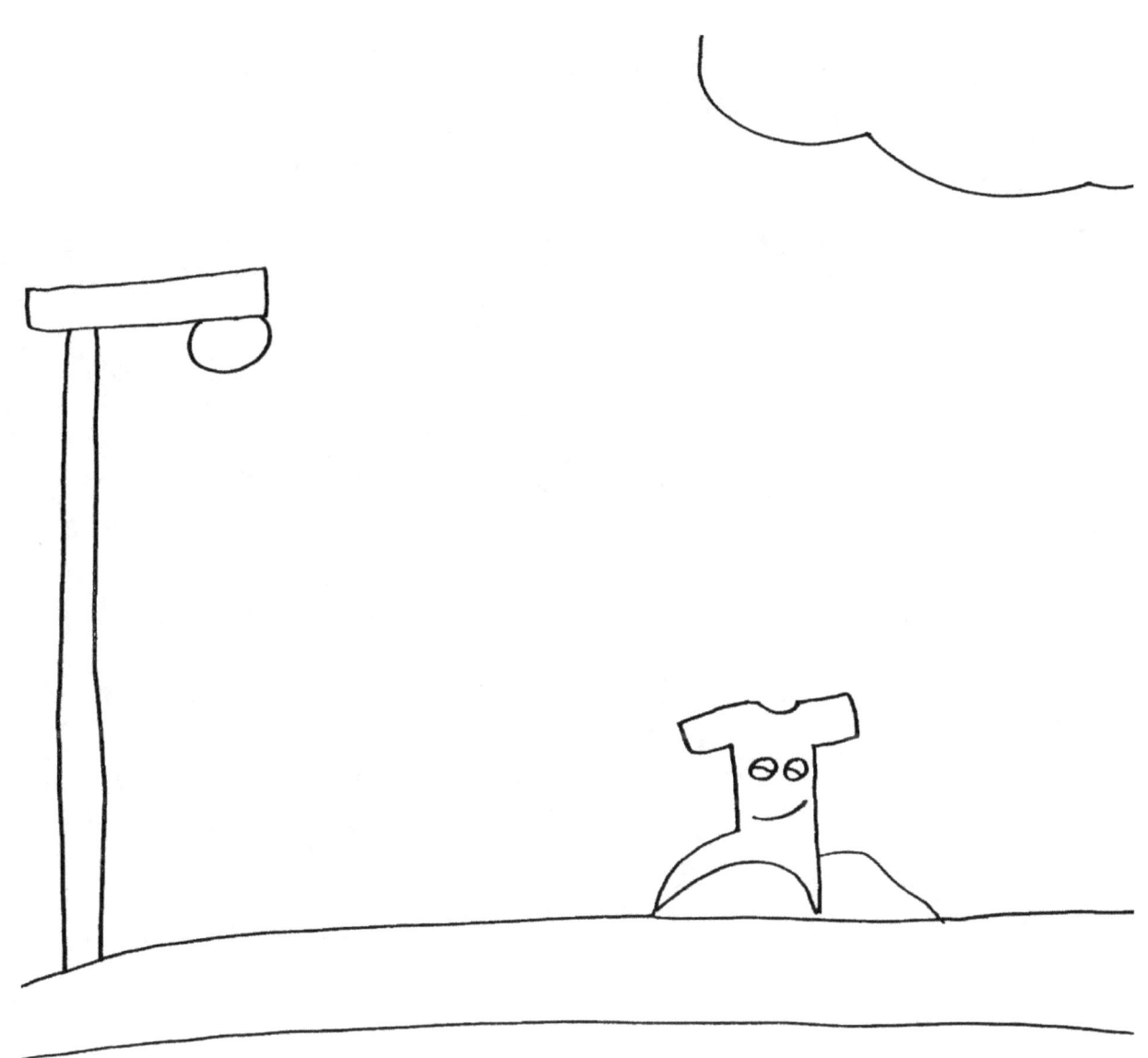

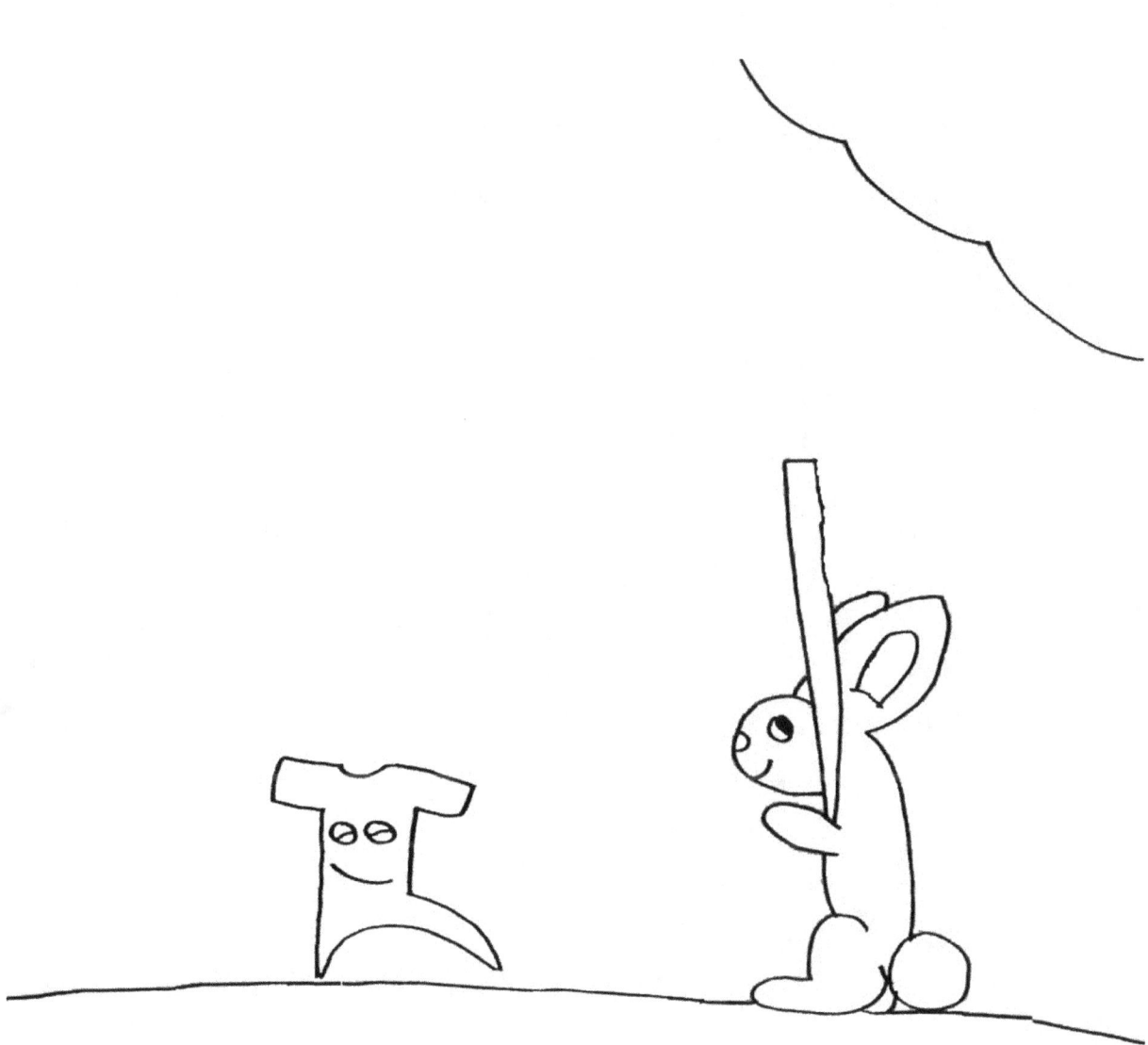

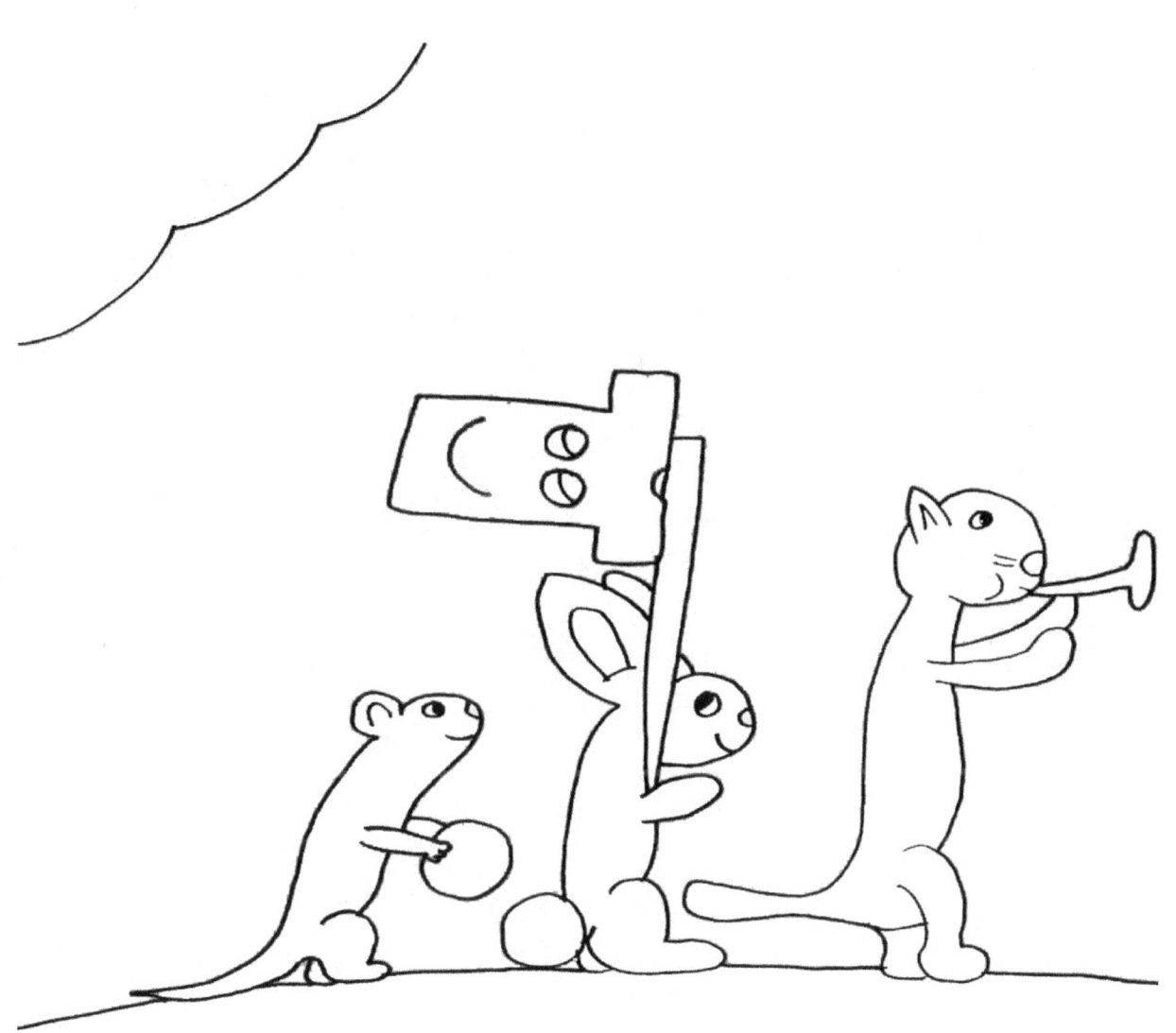